The Ambulance Box

ANDREW PHILIP was born in Aberdeen in 1975 and grew up near Falkirk. He lived in Berlin for a short spell in the 1990s before studying linguistics at Edinburgh University. He has published two poetry pamphlets with Happen*Stance* Press—*Tonguefire* (2005) and *Andrew Philip: A Sampler* (2008)—and was chosen as a Scottish Poetry Library 'New Voice' in 2006. *The Ambulance Box* is his first book of poems.

Also by Andrew Philip

POETRY CHAPBOOKS
   Tonguefire (HappenStance, 2005)
   Andrew Philip: A Sampler (HappenStance, 2008)

The Ambulance Box

ANDREW PHILIP

for Pip & Katie,

with love,

Andrew Philip

SALT

LONDON

PUBLISHED BY SALT PUBLISHING
Fourth Floor, 2 Tavistock Place, Bloomsbury, London WC1H 9RA United Kingdom

Salt Publishing 2009
Paperback edition 2010

Printed and bound in the United Kingdom by Lightning Source UK Ltd

Typeset in Swift 9.5 / 13

ISBN 978 1 84471 491 9 hardback
ISBN 978 1 84471 762 0 paperback

1 3 5 7 9 8 6 4 2

for Aidan Michael Philip
born and died

4 September 2005

Contents

Acknowledgements

Acknowledgements are due to the editors of the following publications and Web sites, where versions of some of these poems first appeared: *A new orkney anthology* (The George Mackay Brown Writing Fellowship, 2008), *Artisan, Chapman, island, Lallans,* www.poetcasting.co.uk, *The Rialto, The SHOp,* www.shorepoets. org.uk, *The Smoky Smirr o Rain* (Itchy Coo, 2003) and *Third Way.*

Several poems in this collection were published in the HappenStance Press pamphlets *Tonguefire* (2005) and *Andrew Philip: A Sampler* (2008).

Wandelvakanties dicht bij huis (*Walking Holidays Close to Home*) is the title of a book by Paul Maes (Uitgeverij Terra-Lannoo, 2003).

The following are translations of poems by Rainer Maria Rilke: 'Hairst Day' ('Herbstag'), 'Orpheus. Eurydice. Hermes.' ('Orpheus. Eurydike. Hermes.') and 'Spanish Dancer' ('Spanische Tänzerin').

'Pilgrim Variations' was written for David Martin's exhibition 'Rumours and Revelations' at the Shore Gallery, Leith, in 2005.

'Still' is a response to Alison Watt's painting of the same title in the memorial chapel of Old St Paul's Episcopal Church, Edinburgh.

Many thanks to Michael Symmons Roberts, David Kinloch and Rob A. Mackenzie for their support and advice.

fo cheò

islands buried in the sky's white sands

Summa

Even the stones cry out.

Even the trees shrapnelled
into leaf and blossom.

Even the cough of dust
shuffling down a blade of sun.

Even the sunlight itself,
the movement of the air,

the gashed and mounded earth.
Even the tripwire heat,

even the hirpled season's
unseasonable crops;

even the implacable greenness
of each field, lawn and brae.

Even this caged
and blootered heart

rattling the bars for freedom—
even it is party

to the gathering cause.

Pedestrian

Someone was standing in the middle of the road.
She stood astride it, just beyond
the blind spot on a sharp, countryside bend,
so hidden that I nearly ran her over.
At first, she seemed an ordinary figure
—jeans, a fitted t-shirt, long brown hair—
but for the confidence with which she stood
where any car would slam straight into her.
Almost as soon as we jerked to a halt
and I got out the car to remonstrate,
the space around her ruptured
with the opening of wings
as colourful as the flocks of paradise.
She stretched her hand towards me, said
I know you'll take good care of it and poured
from her palm into mine a sleeping child,
scarcely the size of a nut and sprouting
from its belly a shoot topped off by a tiny leaf.
I tried to ask the obvious questions, but she
folded herself from our vision.
I felt her gift stir slightly, though it slept
as soundly as it does now in my hand.
How can I drive on with this entrusted to me?
I'm rooted here, keeping watch
on the growth of what is planted in my palm—
this difficult, unasked-for joy.

Triptych

I. HIS WADING LIGHT

after Rembrandt's
'The Flight into Egypt: A night piece'

Keep moving!—I say to myself—*Keep*
moving: by daybreak, we need to be
far from where we started and are now.
Never was I so scared of the dark:
this night's that solid, the trees, bushes
and rocks seem made of the gloom. Never
was a light so heavy as the one
I'm carrying. How can I keep it
from spilling itself into the world?
I used to know where I was with God.
I knew—even through all her visions
and that first strange dream of mine—until
I held the bairn, steadying his head
like it's the last nail for my coffin.

II. A Voice is Heard in Ramah

I have to trust him now:
his dreams and sense of direction:

we heard the death squads and screams
as we stole out the town,

the smashed doors
and fruitless attempts to resist,

the inconsolable mothers sobbing
and the exhausted silences of their men.

We could hear it all for ages
as we picked our way over rocks and scrub.

Hardly a word has passed between us since.
What could we say with all that behind us

and knowing that our boy—my boy—
the boy I huddle, feed and coorie doun—

is the one they are after,
the cause of all that death?

III. DOWN DARKNESS WIDE

Enough light to see by. I don't want
enough light to see by, not if this
is all I can see. How could we know
we were harbouring a fugitive
among our infants before those beasts
lit torches at the town's edge and tore
the deep black veil from our streets and homes?
By then, it was too late. Now, I am
a man twice my age and adding years
every tiny grave we dig. It's said
the one they wanted missed the slaughter:
may the father perish well before
the son's majority, the mother
live the grief we owe to her offspring's
presumption to be born as one of us.

Wandelvakanties Dicht bij Huis

I.

IN SIGHT

We stopped in our tracks—
someone flicked on the poppies,
squinted at us down
the length of dyke we trod, down
the long-barreled afternoon.

II.

BIRD LIFE ON THE MARCH TO ARNHEM

A stork fled the calm.
Perhaps it saw them coming,
those rains that caught us
marching the edge of the field
to the call *Strengthen! Strengthen!*

III.

IT WAS ON A DAY SUCH AS THIS

A wave of barley.
Poplars painted on thin air.
The light cracks like paint—
a twig beneath a jackboot—
a mind beneath the white lamp.

Child of Calmer Waters

for Noah Nicholson

Child of calmer waters, you come
after the storm.

May your tongue be
the olive branch in the dove's beak.

May dry land always be granted:
a firm place

to set your foot:
a clear but unfamiliar stride to take.

Singularity

I imagine the universe
hefted

in the hands of God
lighter even

than you will be
little hoard of brightness

when you come
squalling into my arms

Hairst Day

Lord: it is time. The simmer gied braw yield.
Lay yer shaddae doun upon the sundials
an lowse the winds ontil the fields.

Command the final fruits tae ful the vine;
gie them twa mair days o southren weather,
push them intil ripenin and pester
the last o sweetness throu the heavy wine.

Them that has nae hous will no can bigg ane nou.
Them that's by their lane has lang tae wait,
tae wauken, read, write muckle letters late,
stravaig the wynds an avenues unquait
when leaves is driftin throu the toun.

The Invention of Zero

What like was it
    this abundant world

where nothing was not—
    no neat ring

shackling us to absence,
    no way not

to count or be counted—
    where everything

filled without this
    empty nest of a number

perched in the mind,
    everything swerved

its wide white oblivion;
    and could we

given the state of our knowledge
    live with the lack of it

unable to quantify
    certain populations

in the wild, the exhaustion
    of our reserves,

the number and intensity
    of cries in the night?

Saxifrage

seed with a sharp eye for the tenderness
that can open a drystane mind

    (sole voice   voting for the impossible
    delicate light   going on in the darkness)

seed that shows how slight is the sustenance
a life can grow from
                       (a life no less

    and yet   never enough)

The Ambulance Box

No one can swear how it fell
into our hands. No one

can fathom its substance or build.
It mystifies all

who think of themselves as whole
but those of us huddled

round our various wounds
are at home with the box

and all it contains.
                    Hear us,
shoulder to shoulder in the dusk,

celebrate life — sprained and splinted
broken
            bandaged
                        set to heal

Cardiac

for Alexander Burrough

You ask the reason why we've just one heart:
dear friend, I am surprised that's not enough.
Perhaps you have forgotten how it's built:
the doubling of each chamber, of each beat,
which means that dialogue and argument
—for all that can be said in detriment
of this—are ever basic to our quick.

And think how heart rates quicken with deceit
as much as with the first gasp of desire.
What separates a lover from a liar
if nothing in the heart? Even the pick
of those we share our pulse with shares this jolt
beneath the ribs, this double click of love.
How could they cope with even one just heart?

45 Minutes

time enough

I listen to my wife and daughter breathing through the night

time enough for three shots at fame

the night that opens round us like the latest film

time enough to travel between certain major cities

a film released to eager crowds across the globe

time enough—or so we were told—for the unthinkable to strike

this globe that shudders through the depths of space

time enough for the hero of the show to avert disaster

the depths we see as the dark between the stars

time enough to dream the outline of a better world

the stars that furnish the dust of our bodies

time enough to be born and to die

these bodies we surrender every moment

time enough to learn that no time is ever enough

Wilderness with Two Figures

Two men sit in open ground.
One holds a watch, the other a trout.
The one who holds the watch
envies the other's contact with nature.

The one who holds the trout
wishes he could tell the time of day.
The watch is battery powered
and there are no shops

within travelling distance. The trout,
naturally, is dead. It is summer
and there is no ice. Not everything
is as simple as it might seem.

The Meisure o a Nation

the tonnage o steel bashed on the Clyde
    minus the rummle o a coal train in the Lithgae nicht

the metres o film anent Mary Queen o Scots
    dividit by a decade's terrestrial variations

the sum o *Chi Mi Na Morbheanna* and *Ebeneezer Goode*

the heicht o a West Lothian shale bing
    ower the ugsomeness o wir apencast mines

Sheena Easton
    tae the pooer o Runrig

the nummer o times Iain Crichton Smith wrote *Cha duirt e smid*

the lang leet o synonyms for *fu*
    dividit by the kenspeckle names naebody kens

the fowk that aw hinks this is written in slang
    agin ilkane o the leids a body can hear in the kintrae

the hunnerwecht o fish landit at a north-east herbour ony day

the crisis o confidence
    minus the ink skailt in blamin John Knox

Kirsty Wark plus Eddie Mair all squared

the freinlyness o the Tartan Airmy
    dividit by a year's renditions o *The Sash*

the memorials for Scotty taen awa fae them for Fergusson

the ile revenues
    plus or minus Bannockburn

the wecht o Davie Hume's absent wig
    taen awa fae the ice aneath the Rev Robert Walker's feet

Dolly the Sheep times the carronade

the area o coast Neil Oliver hasnae stravaiged
    times the distance wir national drink has traivelt

the Darien fleet
    dividit by Miralles's whummlit boats

Oor Wullie times *Trainspotting* times the *Drunk Man* times *Taggart*

Man with a Dove on his Head

The man next door has a dove on his head.
He can't remember how it got there,
but those who've seen the evidence suspect
it hatched amongst his springy curls.
We don't know where he goes each Wednesday,
but he returns cooing to the bird and streets.
Although he's used to stares, the giggles,
taunts and nicknames scunner him. We ask
about support groups, fellow sufferers
and those who've come through the condition.
He says, *This dove is here for the duration,*
and tells us: *There are far more than you realise*
who wander round with a bird on their heads —
a dove, a parrot, magpie, rook or hawk.

In Answer to the Question

    i.   Something about the angle of a given corner.

    ii.   Because a word—say, *blackberry*—hangs over the border.

    iii.   *But it just fell apart in my hands,* he said.

    iv.   From not allowing martins to build nests.

    v.   Something about a bruised fruit, weeping.

    vi.   For failure to see the dogrose.

    vii.   The slow drip in the mind saying   *hunt*   *hunt*   *hunt.*

The Image of Gold and the Fiery Furnace

The demand to serve;
the demand to be faithful—

    to keep our heads in a hostile state,
    to keep our names in a country

that stamps us like another bail of cotton.
The need to keep the language of that state

    smart and comfortable like the coats
    we wear around the town or court

and yet to wear the torn, patched
language of our childhood

    clean and bright beneath it all.

The command to obey;
the command not to obey

    the codes we've followed
    our whole lives through—

to kneel to something we recognise only
as a risible blasphemy fit for the cowp.

    The need to speak—to speak up and out—
    to speak a mind that's set

firmer than the bricks and mortar of the palace
louder than the sound

of the horn, flute, zither, lyre and harp
to speak it with a heat that sears

like the furnace at whose mouth we stand defiant
but speak without the singe of disrespect.

To speak as if our lives depended on it.

sligean air an traigh

all the bonnier for being *briste   briste   briste*

Pilgrim Variations
for David Martin

I. THE DEPARTURE BOARD

If it's your avowed intent, go on then: leave
and live among us

separately. Laden like that, you can forget
a swift departure for all

your talk of high-speed links to yonder
wicket gate.

If you're after a haven, you're looking
for the last orchid

on a vast and inhospitable hillside.
If you're searching

for a sense of everything set right, you're on
a wild goose chase.

Is that what you want? Is that really all it means
to be a pilgrim?

II. Escape Velocity

Trajectory orbit velocity   course:
   these, Pilgrim, are

the focus of my labour   the factors I strive
   to better

understand manipulate plan
   that we might

fulfil what I deem to be our duty:
   to reach

the end of air resistance
   and break

free of the weight that binds us
   to earth,

the afterburn of Goddard's rocket
   turning our ties

to surface—land and water—to history
   to ash.

III. To the Naked Eye

Who can restrain the urge to look?
After all, that's what you came here for
without caring for the first principle of optics.
Light is the eye's admission, travelling further
than either of us can imagine, unaware
of you, me, distance, circumstance
or the sense of something shared it might create
shining on the righteous and unrighteous.
Look me in the eye. What do you see:
the lamp of the body? the wind's eye to the soul?
Much less, I'd guess, than when you stare
up into the night sky, which hides as much
as it reveals to naked eyes like ours.

iv. Eschatology for Dummies

What do you think's to be gained by getting
close, Pilgrim? Keep going; keep your distance.
So what if you reckon your resistance
is strong enough to stand the pull? Guessing's
neither safe nor sound, but in these last
shudders and gasps of this gutter planet
where your feet have found you—please don't panic—
the guessing game is all we've not yet lost.
People always itch to see a sign,
especially those who're keen to get things sussed.
I don't know what's behind this door, but I'm
pretty sure you wouldn't want it loose.
Perhaps it's preordained, has reached its time.
Perhaps it's just a matter of free choice.

v. ICE-BOUND

Bitterer lesson cannot be than that
there are paths and paths
and the one you're on is the worst.

The number of times I've started off
and though my hopes were up
have found myself lost again, out

among sub-zero blankness.

And you, Pilgrim, with your cocksure
sense of direction and sacrifice,
you think you'll get me to look

you in the eye. No chance, but if
you'd care to follow, I'll show you.
Just step outside with me into

the perfect drift and freeze.

VI. No Thread to Follow

Searching for the way up and out?
You might be in for a surprise.
Looking for the way to the centre?
There's no thread to follow, Pilgrim, so
sharpen your sense of direction and choose
remembering each fork in the road
you've come to and resolved.
They say there is a route that seems
right to a man. They say the way up
is the way down. They say nothing
is the new left and right. So beautifully,
they say   choice is agony.

VII. FUTUROLOGY

Open empty unblemished unadorned:
the future   (*Was that a knock at the door?*)   is here.

You don't believe me, Pilgrim?
   (*There's somebody at the door.*)

Perhaps you're looking in the wrong direction.
   (*There's somebody at the door.*)

Perhaps your heart is in the wrong place.
   (*Knock, knock. Never at quiet.*)

Perhaps, for all the miles you've covered
   (*I stand at the door and knock.*)

there's a part of you unwilling to rise
above the comfort of yourself.

   (*I stand at the door and knock.*)
Grab your coat and get your hat:

   (*Knock, knock. Never at quiet.*)
it's about time.

VIII. FIRE STORM

The bright wind scatters all
you believe
        everything you thought

you knew and trusted.
There's no eye to this storm. It can't be

avoided with weather charts
        battened down against

at home   or in some civic shelter
but whether you survive, Pilgrim,

is down to you.
        Can you feel
its igneous breath on the back of your neck?

        Es ist Zeit

believe and be baptised.

IX. VIA NEGATIVA

What did you expect: a haven, a mansion;
two fish suppers or a bottle and loaf;
a genuine, old-style resurrection?
Were you expecting the usual clim-

ax to a day's hard graft; a new equation;
a Hubble shot of open space
in the morning paper; a deep occlusion
of what you knew to be the truth?

Did you expect a set of directions—
the straight and narrow; an empty path?
Pilgrim, did you expect to breeze right in?

Hands up who can restrain the urge to laugh:
this is the door you have to pass
through but can't. Not yet. Not while I'm game.

x. The Welcoming Committee

It might be that you want to pray here.
If so, feel free to kneel among the debris and the ash.

It might be that you want to dance.
If you can find an unencumbered space, then go ahead.

Perhaps you feel the urge to sing among these broken walls.
I'd join you, but I don't have much voice left.

Does it surprise you, Pilgrim, that I
should grow as hoarse as this?

It doesn't do to shout too much above the sounding brass.
Better to bide your time for quiet or seek

some resonant space—say, a railway station hall
where your *Erbarme Dich* can echo

down the platforms and the tracks to find
an ear bled open by the silence.

solus na stoirme

where sky and land split   a fragment of grief flickers

Still

this quartered world

              stunned into mourning

    for itself

   ~

after clinical tautness

            the rucked

    winding

          sheet

   ~

that cradled absence

            living amongst us

    waxing

   ~

he is not here

       he is not here

    he is

            not here

Improvisation for the Angel
Who Announces the End of Time

i.m. Olivier Messiaen

one foot on the sea and one on the land

one foot on the rising sea and one on the withering land

    (and the birds

one foot on famine and pestilence, one foot on drought

one foot on the polar meltwaters, one foot on peak oil

    (and the birds in the tree

one foot on the grave and one on the death of the grave

one foot on *Lord, Lord* and one on *Today you will be with me*

    (and the great abundance

one foot on the immortality and one on the eternity

one foot on the celestial city, dressed as a bride, and one to follow

    (and the great abundance
                      of birds in the tree —

one foot on judgment, one foot on all things made new

one foot on the canyons and one on the stars

(and the great abundance
                of birds in the tree of life—

what song
          what song
                    what song

Berlin / Berlin / Berlin
for Maggie Werner

Heute keine Schlagzeile.

As if seein history for the first time.

On the S-Bahn, the construction wirker sittin anent me transmogrified
  intae an exylt Scot.

Potsdamer Platz in atween.

Die Wilmersdorfer Witwen.

PDS posters in the streets aroun Hauptbahnhof.

At Turkish coffee, reid wine and poetry, the connections atween wir
  vocabularies stairtit tae unfauld.

In the *Hochhausvierteln*, the high-rise flats wis aw
  that dreich and uniform.

For a German shop tae be cried 'McPaper' felt like a personal insult.

I wis telt maist o the green postdatit the oncome o capitalism.

Gänseschmalz. Mohnkuchen. Pfefferminztee. Rauschgift.

Döner kebabs wi braw Turkish breid and sauces.

He wis English and cuidnae hear the difference atween
  schwul and *schwül.*

She wis American and cuidnae hear the difference atween
  Höhle and *Hölle.*

»Wenn man die taz als Lektüre nimmt . . .«

He pushed his hydrocephalic son doun the cairrage,
    cadgin cash for the laddie's operation.

The langsomeness o the Palast der Republik.

Ostalgie amang freins.

Arbeiterwohnkasten.

Aside the neo-Nazi graffiti, graffiti fae the Edelweiss Pirates.

Efter sneckin his satchel fae the clashin door,
    he daunert doun the cairrage singin an aria.

She stuid in a quait side street efter 1 in the mornin,
    waitin on the pedestrian lights turnin green.

The official dealin wi ma paperwark shut the door tae
    his office and pechit: *Wissen Sie, das ist ein scheiß Job.*

Heute kein Kommentar.

Smilin, she stuck her heid throu a hole in the Waw.

Construction. Construction awgaits. Construction at ilka level.
    Construction like ye widnae credit.

Ist das die alte Bibel? an auld boy on the S-Bahn speirt o me.

Chynge at Rosa Luxemburg Platz.

For the benefit o the cairrage, she mutterit calumnies
anent the Slavs.

Orte des Schreckens die wir niemals vergessen dürfen.

KaDeWe.

When Linie U1 resumit its run throu tae Warschauer Straße it
wis like a gala day.

The ainly books on his shelf: the complete warks o Marx,
abridged.

Up afore the day-daw queuein for a place in
the official queue.

»Zoooooooooologischer Garten!«

Coronach

The deid breakfast quait-like at wir table.
They tak their saits afore we're waukent,
waitin sounless on a taste o warmth.

They cleek us by wir airms tae talk aboot
the afairs o daith, strauchlin tae fin
a caller vyce. We hae nocht tae say

tae the deid—nocht or ower muckle:
mair nor a bodie can bear tae speak oot
mair nor a word or a life can haud—

syne we sit an listen day efter day
ettlin for the wee bit word that'll gar
the stounin in wir herts devaul,

an the deid bide anent us in wir kitchen,
their whisperin vyces a souch o pain,
a seasonless smirr on the gless.

Orpheus. Eurydice. Hermes.

Yon wis the unco mine o sowels.
As quait as siller ure, they veined the mirk.
Atween the roots, kythed the burnheid o the bluid
that flows tae aw Jock Tamson's bairns, and hit
looked heavy in the mirk, like porphyry.
Nocht else wis reid.

There wis craigs
and wuids that kent nae craiturs. Brigs ower tuimness
and yon muckle, grey, blin lochan
that hung faur abuin its grund
like rain-fult heivins hingin ower a landscape.
And in atween the meedows, douce and fu o let-be,
the ae path's peelie-wally strip appeared,
a line o linen laid oot lang tae bleach.

Alang this ae path wis the wey they cam.

In front, the spirlie man in his blae mantle,
tongue-tackit and impatient, keeked oot aheid.
His steps ate up the path in muckle bites
but didnae chow; his heavy, steikit neives
hung fae the faw o the mantle's faulds
and didnae ken the clarsach ony mair
that wis ingrown intil his left the wey
that roses grows amang the olive brainches.
His senses seemed as if they were in twae:
like a dug, his sicht wid rin aheid o him,
birl roun, come back and, time and again, staun
waitin at the path's neist bend,
but his hearin wid bide roun him like a smell.

Whiles, it seemed tae him tae rax the hail road
back tae the steps o thae twa ither bodies
that shuid be follaein the hail ascent.
Syne, whit wis ahint him wis nae mair nor
the echo o his climbin and his mantle's flap.
But he still telt hissel they were aye comin;
said it loud and heard it go unheedit.
O ay, they cam, but thae twa wis
fell quait in gaun. Gin he cuid turn and look
juist the yince (gin keekin back widnae mean
the malafoosterin o this hail wark,
that wisnae yet completit), he wid see them,
baith the twa quait fowk that follaes sounless:

the god o errants, the god that taks news faur,
his traivelin bunnet sittin ower bricht een,
his spirlie staff held oot afore hissel
the peerie wings flichterin at his ankles;
and his left haun wis gied tae: her.

The lassie that belovit, that ae clarsach
gied oot mair yammer nor ony yammer-weemin;
that a warld wis makkit oot o yammer, whaur
a bodie cuid find awthing: buss and glen
and wey and toun, field and burn and baest;
and that aroun yon yammer-warld, juist like
aroun the ither yird, a sun
and a sternfu, silent heivin gaed,
a yammer-heivin wi distorit sterns—
This lassie that belovit.

But she gaed wi her haun in yon god's haun,
lang windin sheets constrictin aw her steps,
unsiccar, cannie, no at aw impatient.
Tint in hersel, like fowk that's howpin muckle,
she didnae think on him that gaed up front
or on the path that taen them up tae life.
She wis tint in hersel. Her state o daith
fult her like abundance.
Like a fruit o sweetness and mirk, she wis fu
o her muckle daith, a daith that wis that new
she didnae unnerstaun a thing.

She wis awa in a new maidenheid
and wis untouchable; her sex wis shut
the wey a young flooer shuts afore the gloamin
an mairrage wis that unco til her hauns,
the licht god's touch—aye quait and leadin on—
gart her grue like something ower fameeliar.

She wis nae mair yon yella-heidit wife
that whiles wis heard o in the poet's sangs,
nae mair the braid bed's scent and island, her;
she wis yon mannie's property nae mair.

She wis awready loosened like lang hair
and gied up like the rain that's fawen doun,
distributit like hunners o supplies.

She wis awready root.

And when, suddenly,
the god stopped her and said thae words wi pain
clear in his vyce: *He's turnt hissel aroun—*
she didnae unnerstaun and quait-like said: *Wha?*

Faur awa, daurk afore the bricht ootgang,
a body stuid, whase coontenance
wisnae tae be kent. He stuid and watched
whit wey, on the strip o a meedow path
the god o errants, wi sorra in his een,
turnt roun wioot a word tae follae yon
that wis awready gaun the ae wey back,
lang windin sheets constrictin aw her steps,
unsiccar, cannie, no at aw impatient.

Waukrife

Come in fae the cauld, man. It's ower late
tae be staunin at the thrashel wi the wind
scrummlin in the corners o wir hous.
There a braw fire burnin.
                              Come awa ben
an tak a drink tae warm yersel.
Yer auld sait's empty an it's no the same
sittin by ma lane at the fire aw nicht.

Hou lang will ye bide like this—
anither month, anither year or mair?
Ye hae tae face the truth:
                              she isnae comin hame.
Yon man o hers turnt out juist as ye said:
guid for naethin but a sang or twa hunner.

Near on every nicht, I'm waukent
fae a vyce warslin wi her name:
Eurydice! Eurydice!—a soun
that roch it gars me hink
                              the vyce is yours
syne I'm turnin ower tae fin
your hauf o the bed cauld as the nicht,
as the smoort fire in the grate.

To Bake the Bread

I care about nothing but baking good bread.
There is my family to feed—and this village.
My wife, she worries that I burn my fingers
when I reach down into the oven.
Better, I say, that I burn my hands
than lose them to the snigger of a mine,
as Rahmat did, who used to work the fields.

It is no life for a man if he can't work.
Better, some say, that you lose your home but still
can eat than that you lose a limb and starve.
Perhaps you call us 'simple' for our ways—
I have heard it said the educated do.
Why wish for a life more complicated
when each day here is difficult enough?

A month or so ago, I had this dream:
The fields were white with grain ripe for the mill.
For miles and miles, a man's eye saw nothing
but the wind ruffling the white hair of the crop.
We men laughed our bellies sore; our women
smiled for the first time since our wedding days:
there would be bread and cakes—and fodder for beasts.

I woke back into our habitual scowls.
The fields were still those scrawny plains and slopes,
those dustbowls where we scratch a tiny yield.
I could tell nobody the dream, of course,
but it returns to me night and again
as if the fields are calling me to speak their dreams
like a prophet pleading a people's case to God.

The mornings find me shy of daylight and my walk
the length of this village to the bakehouse stores,
half hoping once again to find them bursting.
Better, I tell myself each step, to bake
my batch of loaves and keep the few alive
than wither in the dream that we've enough
to bake the bread for all my countrymen.

Tonguefire Night

MacAdam rakes up the tongues
of men, women and a handful

of angels from where they've fallen
their coppers and golds layered

on his path, lawn, borders
and vegetable patch:

he knows that if
he cowps them on the compost heap

they might in time reveal
his father's speechgifted voice

he buys firelighters and matches
cheap beer and lifestyle magazines

smoke and crackle drift
over the garden wall

the scent of baking apples
mouthwaters from the kitchen:

~

MacAdam sits alone
in the dark with a single malt

while the streetlamps beg admittance
through the trees outside his window

a bairn's cry bursts through his home
startles the crystal in his hand

he checks each room, each cupboard
the dusts of cellar and attic—

all blank   the cry returns:

he scours the garden shed
searches under trees and bushes

pulling apart the compost heap
he discovers, kicking and bawling

in the ashes of his tonguefire,
a baby made of glass:

~

MacAdam holds the bairn
in his guddle of arms

it's cold as ice and won't stay still
it's glass-hard and won't stop girning

he rakes for a blanket
to wrap the child in

sits down and swaddles the bairn
in front of his livingroom fire

sorting skelfs of lullaby
and crooning roughly

into the translucent face
which gradually demists into

a hall-of-mirrors portrait—
his warts-and-all features:

~

MacAdam, who is not expecting post,
finds a sizeable parcel at his door

no one about, and the package
is giving nothing away

he bends to lift it, but the parcel
is much too heavy for anyone

to heft and carry ben:
despite the fear of unpleasant surprises

from imaginary enemies
he resolves to open it and see inside

it's empty—bar a note that says
For yersel and the bairn

and a small, delicate book of songs
bound in white heather

with its vague but unshakeable
sense of shame and longing:

MacAdam swallows
the book of songs

it tastes as sweet as everything
he's prone to forget to praise

but a sourness kicks him
in the pit of his stomach

if this is the cost, he's far from certain
he wants to be the one to pay it:

his tongue thins to a standard
flapping against the roof of his mouth

his heart churns like a Bon Accord lorry
slowing on the brae

his harns and eyes bleeze
with a vision of the mucklegrown bairn:

∾

MacAdam wakes in a hospital bed singing
a tirade of love songs

in a language yet to be born

Dream Family Holiday

We were together, the four of us:
the bay had its arms around us
and the sea whispered towards us

the sun grinned over us
gulls and gannets laughed with us
and the sand sighed at us.

Then I woke up: one of us
still slept, one was gone from us
and one had not yet come to us.

Spanish Dancer

The wey a matchstick in the haun—that's white
afore it bursts in flame—spits oot wild tongues
aw airts, her roun dance, gleg an glowin het,
begins tae braiden oot itsel amang
the crood that circles close aroun her yet.

An on a suddenty, it's aw ae flame.

Wi ae keek syne she kinnels aw her mane
an birls her hail dress wi a daurin skeel
intil this muckle fire, whaur bare airms wheels
awauk an clackin, like snakes that's sair afeart.

An syne: as if the fire cam ower near,
she bunnles it an hurls it on the grund
gey heidie-like, flicks up her pridefu hauns
an keeks: there it's lyin ragin on the flair
still flashin oot an hingin on tae life—.
But shair o winnin, siccar an wi a sweet
smile o kennin, she hauds her face up heich
an stamps it oot wi peerie, solid feet.

Lullaby

this is the arm that held you
this is the hand that cradled your cold feet

these are the ears that heard you
whimper and cough throughout your brush with light

this is the chest that warmed you
these are the eyes that caught your glimpse of life

this is the man you fathered—
his voided love, his writhen pride and grief

The Road from Emmaus

Didn't our hearts burn within us
while he talked with us on the road?

And suddenly as he came
he disappears
                    leaving us

like timbers   glowing after conflagration
apt at any moment
                    to collapse

or red-hot iron   hammered into shape
aware that
                as we cool
                        we harden.

In Question to the Answers?

1. Have you arrived at something yet?

2. Are what and how not entirely clear?

3. Is it, in fact, some *thing*?

4. Does this unnerve you?

5. What is the weather like at your destination?

6. Whose understudy are you?

7. Tonight, I will be mostly wearing . . . what?

8. Are you, in fact, entirely clear?

9. What is the next line in this sequence?

10. Is it something entire?

11. Have you arrived at your destination yet?

12. Does the weather unnerve you?

13. Whose understudy will be most wearing tonight?

14. Is the next lie in this sequence clear?

15. Are you, in fact?

16. Is it safe to go out alone?

17.   Does this unnerve you?

18.   Is it, mostly, the same thing?

19.   How have you arrived at this?

20.   Have you an understudy for tonight?

21.   How safe is the weather to go out in alone?

22.   Does this lie unnerve you?

22.   Who set this understudy alight?

23.   What is most likely to ensue in the silence?

Notes to Self

His eyes opened
the way a packed lift opens on a floor

without a soul leaving
or entering.

~

Beautiful—
a simple entry in the lexicon.

Who would have thought it capable
of such cruelty?

~

One room
still glows with sunlight

as if all the waiting
was over.

~

He opened his eyes
the way you might unlock the door at dusk

on sensing that a certain car has turned
the corner.

~

The agony is not
in the knowing or not knowing   whether

but in the knowing or not knowing
who.

~

Affect of youth
inversely proportionate

to the force events exert
on a body.

~

Did you expect
not to be among the cloven and sundered?

Even the brain is split into
unequal halves.

~

This is your story,
this being splintered   this being

reconstituted, this is
your song.

~

The whole earth
is your charnel house   and here you are

with fresh stones and flowers for
a single grave.

~

Everything is distance,
the artifice involved in this no more

or less than each breath further
away from him.

~

His eyes were open
for the time it takes to strip life back

to the rough, essential moving parts
some want hidden.

~

What nears
the depth of living needed

to account for such
unending—

~

To feel young again—
but what's the point of that obsession?

Better to feel an age freshened
in her smile.

~

Stretch out
your hands: what and who and how

they held and hold cannot be
unheld.

~

Given her grin
and the particulars of her eyes,

why keep looking for that dead
in this living?

~

If you forget
that you came here on a line of song,

look out and up, look hard into the deep,
unshouldered blue.

In Praise of Dust

for Judith

Dust burns in the black lamp beside our bed
  a stale tang seeping through the room.

Breathe in: you will become
an intimate of dust
  conversant with whatever currents keep it
sifting through our air
               in all its mix

of quick and dead: our former pelts
the pollen count
         the air pollution index

10 million square feet of office space
folding on itself
         live on every station.

On this of all days, let's not forget
the facts:
         from dust we are
to dust we are returning.   In between

our substance is less certain:
  a trick of chemistry
           gospel
and perhaps the light

from the black lamp that burns beside our bed
falling on your
       spirited   breathing
muscle and skin.

còmhradh a' chladaich

after all this time, what has the beach left to say to the tide?

Notes

The Gaelic titles of the 'Hebridean Thumbnails' translate as: 'mist-covered', 'shells on the beach', 'storm light' and 'the shore's conversation'; *briste* (pronounced *breesh-chih*) is the Gaelic for 'broken'.

Chi Mi Na Morbheanna ('I see the great mountains') is a well-known Gaelic song of exile. *Cha duirt e smid* means 'He didn't say a word.'

A glossary with the basic intended meanings of the Scots words used in the poems can be found on http://www.andrewphilip.net/ For pronunciation, as well as further meanings and nuances, readers are encouraged to consult a good Scots dictionary, such as the comprehensive online *Dictionary of the Scots Language*, which can be accessed for free at http://www.dsl.ac.uk/dsl/

Lightning Source UK Ltd.
Milton Keynes UK
31 March 2011

170190UK00001B/43/P